Diane McCurry

I worked with Effie at Project CAR
in Sioux Falls in 1991-92. She was
a volunteer & a part time employee. She
was also a wonderful Christian who
lived her faith in every area of her life.

"The Word" Surprises

"The Word" Surprises

Effie Ruth Larson

Diane,
Be stirred &
enriched by He
God's Word as He
blesses your surprises!
Effie Ruth Larson

VANTAGE PRESS
New York

FIRST EDITION

Copyright © 1995 by Effie Ruth Larson

Published by Vantage Press, Inc.
516 West 34th Street, New York, New York 10001

Manufactured in the United States of America
ISBN: 0-533-11473-X

Library of Congress Catalog Card No.: 95-90182

0 9 8 7 6 5 4 3 2 1

In memory of the late Rev. Dr. Norman G. Anderson, who was senior pastor of Saint Stephen's Lutheran Church, West Saint Paul, Minnesota, during the use of the daily Dial-A-Devotion. Reverend Anderson conducted a sign-off on KSTP-TV in the Twin Cities for twenty-five years.

Contents

Foreword

May these devotions encourage you on your walk with God on the journey of your life.

Step by step with another, we become known to each other and are connected in a relationship. No longer strangers, we have a sense of belonging as a child feels in a family.

This poem, "Step By Step," connects me personally with my grandmother who gave it to me. Although the author is unknown, it has become a part of my daily life's walk with God.

Step By Step

He does not lead me year by year
   Nor even day by day
But step by step my path unfolds
   My Lord directs my way.

Tomorrow's plans I do not know
   I only know this minute
That He will say, "This is the way"
   By faith now walk ye in it.

And I am glad that it it so
   Today's enough to bear
And when tomorrow comes, His grace
   Shall far exceed its care.

What need to worry then or fret?
   The God who gave His Son
Holds all my moments in His hands
   And gives them one by one.

As you read Effie's collection of devotions may they help you to go step by step with the Father of us all.

In Christ's love.

—Wanda Todd

Introduction

The Holy Scriptures, the Bible, is often called "the Word." No other book can compare to it because it is God's Word.

It is a fascinating book and these devotions are based upon it. The Bible is full of surprises as you read it. It surprises us when we find a word in it that we didn't think would be there. Many of these devotions are titled by such a surprise word.

The Bible surprises us too because "the Word" is spoken of as a person. "In the beginning, was the Word, and the Word was with God, and the Word was God" (John 1:1). "And the Word became flesh and dwelt among us, full of grace and truth; we have beheld His glory, glory as of the only Son from the Father" (John 1:14).

This Word Who became flesh is Jesus. This Jesus Who turns out to be the Christ is full of surprises. It is hoped that these devotions will pique your curiosity for biblical discovery. Read the Word and grow.

The Scripture passages quoted are from the Revised Standard Version (1952) unless otherwise designated.

Reverence for God is preserved by capitalizing pronouns, including Who, You, Your, Yours, which refer to Him.

"The Word" Surprises

1

Declaration of Dependence on God (Rom. 13: Christian conduct in relation to the state)

On July 4, 1976, the United States of America celebrated the two hundredth anniversary of our Declaration of Independence, July 4, 1776. Did you know or do you now know that a year before our Declaration of Independence we had a Declaration of Dependence on God?

The Continental Congress set aside Thursday the 20th day of July 1775 as a day of public humiliation, fasting, and prayer. Thus, a Thursday in July of 1775 became the first Day of Prayer, uniting the people of the scattered colonies and their Declaration of Dependence on God.

In the Congressional Record of Thursday, June 12, 1975, Mr. Albert Quie of Minnesota states that an often unnoted "Declaration" had been brought to his attention. This was done by the late Rev. N. G. Anderson, then pastor of Saint Stephen's Lutheran Church of West Saint Paul. Consequently, Pres. Gerald R. Ford, in anticipation of the celebration of our Bicentennial in 1976, called for a National Day of Prayer on Thursday, July 24, 1975. President Ford in his proclamation made reference to the Declaration of Dependence on God proclaimed by the Continental Congress in 1775. So the two hundredth anniversary of that day was observed the year before our Bicentennial celebration.

We are a nation on record as trusting in God. We must continue to be that nation.

Kind Heavenly Father, we thank You for these United States of America. Forgive us our sins as a nation and draw us to You that we might honor and glorify the Kingdom of Righteousness. Amen.

2

Chosen
(John 15:16)

When we were children, we often participated in various games in which teams were chosen. How we longed to be chosen at the beginning of the selection. How terrible to feel we weren't good enough or weren't wanted. When chosen we did all we could to let it be known we were good enough. Then the next time around, we might be among the first to be chosen.

As Christians we have been chosen. Jesus says He has chosen us. We were made citizens of the Kingdom at baptism (our second birth). We need to observe and celebrate that birthday. Do you know your baptism date, your spiritual birthday?

In our catechism, by Dr. Martin Luther, we confess in the explanation to the third article: "I believe that I cannot by my own reason or strength believe in Jesus Christ my Lord, or come to Him, but the Holy Spirit has called me by the Gospel."

How wonderful to be chosen! With Jesus we don't have to worry about being good enough. He chooses us through the work of the Holy Spirit and makes a change in our life. One of our hymns states:

When Jesus comes, oh, blessed story
He works a change in heart and life.

We should thank our parents and sponsors who brought us to the font so that we could be born anew and be given spiritual life. They and the church have nurtured that life.

Thank You, Jesus, for choosing us and giving us new life. Live out Your life in and through us so that we bear fruit to Your honor and glory. Amen.

3

Mine!
(Isa. 43:1–3, John 17)

From the time we are little children, we use the word *mine*. We often see little children clinging to a toy and saying, "Mine." This is not all bad even though we often teach a child to share.

As we grow older, there may be much that we say is "mine." My education, my job or position, my house, my car, my good name. This is not to be frowned on either. God wants us to be good stewards of His gifts to us. God also has asked us to help our neighbor to protect his property, his living, and his good name!

How thankful we can be that God also uses the word "mine." In Isaiah, He says, "Fear not, for I have redeemed you—I have called you by name, you are mine." At baptism we were given this spiritual birth and claimed as one of God's children.

In His high priestly prayer in John 17, Jesus prays, "All Mine are Thine, and Thine are Mine and I am glorified in them . . . Holy Father, keep them in Thy Name, which Thou hast given Me, that they may be one even as We are one."

To Thee, Thou bleeding Lamb,
I all things owe,
All that I have and am, and all I know.
All that I have is now no longer mine,
And I am not mine own; Lord I am Thine.
—C. E. Mudie, 1872 LH #398

Lord Jesus, thank You for calling us as Yours. Help us appreciate all we have in You. Amen.

4

His Hand upon Me (Ezra 7:28, Acts 11:21, Ezek. 3:22, Rev. 1:17–18, Ezra, 8:22)

Ezra, priest and scribe, was commissioned by Artaxerxes, King of Persia, to return to Jerusalem together with other Israelite exiles from Babylon. Knowing the hand of the Lord was upon him, Ezra gets the people to bind themselves to the Law of God and successfully accomplishes the mission given by his king.

How thankful we can be that the hand of God has been upon many saints of the past. We think of those in Bible times. Going beyond that, how thankful we can be that the hand of God was upon Dr. Martin Luther during the Reformation and the Renaissance as well as the other reformers.

The hand of our God was certainly upon many who first settled in America. We praise and thank Him for His leading in the great settlement and westward trek in this land.

But the Scripture says: "The hand of our God is upon all who seek Him." Have you known God's hand upon you? Have you been seeking Him daily, asking for His leading and guidance? Do you sing with the hymn writer, "I know the Lord, I know the Lord has laid His hand on me."

Kind Heavenly Father, thank You for laying Your hand on us claiming us as Your own. Keep us in Your hand—never let us go. Amen.

5

Walk
(Lev. 26:3, Ps. 56:13, Isa. 9:2, 30:21, 40:31, Mic. 6:8, John 12:35, Acts 9:31, Rom. 6:4, Gal. 5:16, Eph. 5:8–10, Rev. 3:4)

The Mayo Clinic in Rochester, Minnesota, has put out a booklet titled, "Walk Your Way to Fitness." It is stated that "walking will give you a better quality of life, healthier body composition, better balance and coordination, improved sleep as well as longer life expectancy."

The Scriptures use the word *walk* often, as can be noted in the passages listed above.

There are many different definitions of the word *walk*. The dictionary states that one way in which the word might be defined is: "To follow a certain course of life or conduct oneself in a certain way."

If a person "walks with God," that person will no doubt experience the fitness described by the Mayo Clinic as well as all the blessings of the Triune God.

O Master, let me walk with You
In lowly paths of service true;
Tell me Your secret; help me bear
The strain of toil, the fret of care.
                    —Washington Gladden, 1836–1918

6

Inheritance
(Num. 27, Gal. 3:28c, Eph. 1:13–14)

In Old Testament times, it was said that only sons of a legal wife had the right of inheritance. By the Mosaic Law, a man's property on his death was divided among his sons, the oldest obtaining double the portion assigned to younger brothers.

There were some daughters who spoke up on their own behalf that they should be entitled to the inheritance left by their father. They stood before Moses, Eleazar, the priest, before the leaders and all the congregation and said, "Why should the name of our father be taken away from his family, because he had no son? Give to us a possession among our father's brethren."

Moses asked the Lord about this. The Lord told Moses that the inheritance left by Zelophehad should pass to his daughters.

In these days there is emphasis on the rights of women, and it may be thought that women of the past would not think of speaking up for themselves.

God has said, "You are all one in Christ JESUS." Because we are one in Christ Jesus, we all have a right to the inheritance provided by God our Heavenly Father. "In Him you also, who have heard the word of truth, the gospel of your salvation, and have believed in Him, were sealed with the promised Holy Spirit, which is the guarantee of our inheritance until we acquire possession of it, to the praise of HIS glory" (Eph. 1:13–14).

Lord, help us to lay claims to this inheritance, which is ours by our birthright—born into the Kingdom by baptism. Amen.

7

Standing By
(John 19:25)

"But standing by the cross of Jesus were His mother, and His mother's sister, Mary the wife of Clopas, and Mary Magdalene."

The disciples of Jesus, except Joseph, had all deserted Him and fled. But Mary, His mother was standing by at the cross. She who had kept and pondered many things in her heart, now no doubt realized the meaning of many things. She stood by her son to the very last of His earthly life.

Many times we may need someone to stand by us. Or many times we may need to be the one to stand by someone else.

At times our prayer might be in the words of a hymn penned by C. A. Tindley:

When the storms of life are raging,
Stand by me
When the world is tossing me
Like a ship upon the sea,
Thou who rulest wind and water
Stand by me.

In the midst of tribulations
Stand by me.
When the hosts of hell assail
And my strength begins to fail
Stand by me.

In the midst of persecution
Stand by me
When my foes in battle array
Undertake to stop my sway
Thou who saved Paul and Silas
Stand by me.

In the midst of faults and failures,
Stand by me
When I do the best I can,
And my friends misunderstand,
Thou who knowest all about me,
Stand by me.

Kind Heavenly Father, thank You for standing by us at all times. Give us grace to stand by others in their need. Amen.

8

Free in Christ

So if the Son makes you free, you will be free indeed.

—John 8:36

True freedom can only be known through Jesus, the Son of the Almighty God. He came to earth to take on flesh and be like unto us. He suffered, died, was buried. But God raised Him from the dead, and He reigns on high to make intercession for us.

At one time I wrote a little verse for a school assignment that expresses this freedom.

Lord, let me live
So close to Thee
That I never give
One thought to be
Proud or famed
Nor by the world claimed,
I would be free.

Jesus said, "If you continue in My Word, you are truly My disciples, and you will know the truth and the truth will make you free" (John 8:31–32).

This freedom is available. Claim it and live in it.

Lord Jesus, thank You for the truth that sets us free. Help us to reveal this truth to others. Amen.

9

Good Eating

Thy words were found, and I ate them, and Thy words became to me a joy and the delight of my heart; for I am called by Thy Name, O Lord, God of hosts.

—Jeremiah 15:16

We hear so much these days about eating the right food to keep physically fit. A pyramid of proper foods has been erected, and we are admonished to follow the suggestions on the pyramid to lead healthy lives. This pyramid appears, for example, on cereal boxes.

Do we eat right to stay spiritually fit? Do we grow in our spiritual life? What can give us stamina? What can give us joy and delight?

Jeremiah has the answer: "Thy words."

It is good to have the milk of the Gospel, but Saint Paul urges growth. To the Corinthians, he wrote: "I fed you with milk, not solid food, for you were not ready for it." He said they were babes in Christ. The writer to the Hebrews writes: "For though by this time you ought to be teachers you need someone to teach you again the first principles of God's Word. You need milk, not solid food . . . solid food is for the mature."

Follow Jeremiah's example and dig into the Word of God. Find the joy of discovery and delight in your findings.

Dear Lord, help us to grow up in our Christian life so that we can experience joy and delight as mature Christians. Amen.

10

Kept
(Josh. 14:10, Isa. 49:8, 2 Tim. 4:7, Rev.
3:10, John 17:11–12, Phil. 4:7, Jude 24,
Ps. 121, John 16:12–15)

Most people are keepers. Most people have kept a lot of picture albums over the years. We also like to keep precious articles made by hand by our mothers. Many people today attend antique shows to seek out what has been kept from the past. Purchases made to be kept in their home include such items as antique furniture, pictures, flower vases, and even many times old kerosene lamps from the past. Collections of special plates are also made.

The keeper guards these articles with great care. They are precious and usually very costly.

God too is a keeper. He kept a remnant of the people of Israel, guarded and led them to the promised land. He kept many of the saints in the Old Testament in the palm of His hand. Jesus speaks of having kept His disciples in God's Name and guarding them. Jesus also gives promises that we will be kept and He prays for us. He also says He will send the Holy Spirit Who will keep us and lead us into the truth.

I am reminded of a hymn written by one of my professors that tells of the Heavenly Father's keeping:

In the Holy Father's keeping,
Sheltered in His strong embrace,
Day by day my soul is resting
In that blood-bought precious place,
Here no evil e'er can harm me,
Here I'm safe from sin and pain;

11

In the Holy Father's keeping
Only peace and love can reign.

—Dr. Samuel Martin Miller (1922)

11

Hallowed Eve
(Rom. 1:16, Acts 4:12, Eph. 1:11–13, John 1:12–13)

That which is holy and sacred has often been taken over by the secular world and desecrated. That is what happened to hallowed eve—the evening before All Saints' Day. It is called Halloween and is filled with goblins, ghosts, witches, all kinds of masks, skeletons, and all kinds of revelry. To make it more palatable for little children, the idea of "tricks or treats" came into being. Now not just little children, but bigger ones come for treats.

Is this what Christian people and even churches should promote? You might say it's something perfectly innocent and fun for children.

Maybe we as Christians should reclaim the evening and make it a "Hallowed Eve." Young people as well as children and parents could gather in our churches to commemorate the effects of the Reformation. Films on Dr. Martin Luther could be shown. Hymns could be sung. Bible games could be played. Bible verses could be shared. There are women in our ELCA who can act out the life of Katie Luther. Certain committees could have fun planning such an evening.

Lord Jesus, help us to take back from the secular world that which we as Christians should celebrate as something set apart and holy. Amen.

12

Thanksgiving versus Pride

Lest when you have eaten and are full, and have built goodly houses and live in them . . . then your heart be lifted up and you forget the Lord your God.

—Deuteronomy 8:11–18

It is good to be able to achieve—to reach our goals. Young people need to be encouraged to set goals and then work to achieve them. It may take study; it may take sacrifices; it may take determination in the midst of difficulties.

Achieving our goals, however, can lead to pride. Moses reminds the Israelites that when they have success, they must not forget the Lord their God Who brought them out of the bondage in Egypt and led them through the wilderness. He tells them to beware lest they say in their hearts, "My power and the might of my hand have gotten me this wealth."

As Americans, we celebrate Thanksgiving Day. Some call it "Turkey Day," and time is spent getting stuffed. Americans need to heed the Word, "lest when you have eaten and are full . . . you forget the Lord your God." It's not wrong to gather as a family of thankful people and enjoy a great dinner, but that should not be the whole emphasis. Thanksgiving Day should find us in our churches thanking and praising God for His abundant blessings to us. If we have prospered, thank Him for giving us the ability, the opportunities, the health and His continued grace.

Kind Heavenly Father, thank You for Your goodness to us. Help us as Americans to be ever mindful of Your grace and mercy and to be thankful to You. Amen.

13

Christian Armor
(Eph. 6:10–20)

During World War II, when citizens of the United States were participating in the war, they had to wear military issue. Those who were in the army had to wear army issue and were not allowed to wear civilian clothing at any time. Soldiers were set apart from civilians. Women who were in the WAC's—Women's Army Corps, which later became part of the army—were issued a summer off-duty dress and a winter off-duty dress. Thus when off duty, they had something to wear other than the regular uniform. Those of us who were in the Medical Corps were also issued hospital dresses to wear while on duty. So we had quite a wardrobe.

As Christians we are in a warfare too, and Saint Paul describes the whole armor of God. We are to take this armor and put it on so that we can withstand evil. Loins are to be girded with truth. The breastplate is righteousness. Feet are to be shod with the equipment of the gospel of peace. The shield of faith can quench the flaming darts of the evil one. Heads are to be protected with the helmet of salvation. The power in our hand is the sword of the Spirit, which is the Word of God. Fully equipped we are to pray at all times. We too are set apart.

Christ our Lord provides this armor, and we must not be found without it in this war against the devil and the forces of evil. Marching forward we can sing, "Onward Christian Soldiers."

Lord Jesus, we thank You for the armor provided. Help us always to be dressed for the fray. May we live in the Word, the sword of the Spirit. Amen.

14

You Can Do This!
(Matt. 6:25–34, John 17, Col. 3:10–14,
Rev. 3:18, Rev. 3:4–5, Isa. 61:10)

A recent TV ad tells us that for a casual look we can put away our jeans for a while and buy some attractive dresses that will be fitting for many occasions. The vivacious woman in the ad says, "You can do this!"

We often think about what to wear. What can I put on today? What is fitting for where I'll go today?

Paul tells us in his writings that the Christian life should be a transformed walk and we should know what to wear. Paul urges us to put on: compassion, kindness, lowliness, meekness, and patience. To be comfortably dressed in the Christian life, do this: if you have a complaint against anyone—forgive. That will make a difference in your appearance. Put on love, let the peace of Christ be a ruling force. Let the Word of Christ dwell in you richly. Teach and admonish one another. Sing psalms and hymns and give thanks. That will enhance your facial expression.

You can do this! Yes, you can do this because you are one of God's chosen ones. Christ, Who died for you, now lives in glory, and intercedes for you. He sends the Holy Spirit to lead and guide you. As Christ sends you into the world, He wants you to be dressed fittingly for all occasions.

Lord Jesus, thank you for letting us know what we are to put on. Help us to follow Your directives. Amen.

15

Forgiveness
(Psa. 32, Isa. 44:22, Isa. 43:25, Matt.
18:21–22, Luke 17:1–6, Gen. 42–50)

A most moving story descriptive of forgiveness is the story of Joseph in the Book of Genesis. Read it again and again. Joseph, who had been ill-treated by his brothers, comes to their rescue when life becomes difficult for them. Forgiveness is there and much action toward his brothers and his father to better their lives and give them many blessings.

Peter, the disciple, once asked Jesus about how many times to be forgiving to a person. Was the law of seven times good enough? Jesus tells him not only seven times but seventy times seven.

There may be many instances in life that seem almost impossible for forgiveness to be extended. But we must forgive. We are just hurting ourselves if we do not forgive. It can become a festering sore.

Think of how God has forgiven us. Hang on to His promises. When the devil tries to defeat you by reminding you of what you have done, tell him God has removed it. As far as the East is from the West so far has He removed our transgressions from us. He has promised that He will not remember our sins because Jesus has paid the penalty for them.

Kind Heavenly Father, we can't begin to thank you enough for forgiveness. Help us to be forgiving to those who sin against us. Amen.

16

Life in His Name
(John 20:30, John 21:25)

The fourth Gospel, written by John, the beloved disciple, a son
of Zebedee, speaks of God as the Word. This Gospel reveals God
who became incarnate as Jesus Christ and lived among people.

John shows that Jesus is the eternal Son of God Who by His
person, His teaching, His miracles, His healing, His death and
resurrection has secured salvation to all who receive Him.

John was a man of deep spiritual insight and loving dispo-
sition. He was one of the three disciples who were the inner circle
of Jesus. No doubt John could have written in more detail about
his experiences, but he couldn't possibly include everything.

John wrote the essentials for us. He states that the world
probably couldn't contain the books if all was to be written about
the things done by Jesus. John says, "These are written that you
may believe that Jesus is the Christ, the Son of God, and that
believing you may have life in His Name." We have in this Gospel
the truth we need. Life—spiritual life is the one thing needful
and it can be ours when we believe.

*Lord Jesus, help us to believe and receive You as the Christ
Who gives us life. Amen.*

17

Pruning
(John 15:1–2)

Jesus has saved us and we believe. We are His because He has chosen us to be His own. "You did not choose Me, but I chose you and appointed you that you should go and bear fruit and that your fruit should abide; so that whatever you ask the Father in My Name, He may give it you" (John 15:16).

As we look at the directives for Christian living as followers of Jesus, we discover that many things need to be pruned away. Think about these things and then pray that He will prune away what is not to be a part of the Christian life.

Study the Book of James to see what is said about the tongue. Study the Sermon on the Mount in Matthew 5, 6, and 7. Study the Book of Romans. Study the Pharisees and Sadducees to see if some of their characteristics, which we think are unwanted, might be plaguing us.

Heavenly Father, pruning might be difficult to take but necessary. Help us to live to glorify You. Amen.

18

Wonderfully Made

I will give thanks unto Thee; for I am fearfully and wonderfully made: wonderful are Thy works.

—Ps. 139:14 (ASV)

Did you ever stop to think what a wonderful mechanism the human body is? The body in many ways can heal itself. Even when it has help from the medical profession, it can work miracles. A doctor may say he has done all he can and will then have to leave it up to God.

How does God want us to view our bodies? Saint Paul writes in 1 Corinthians 6:19 and 20: "Do you not know that your body is a temple of the Holy Spirit within you, which you have from God? You are not your own; you were bought with a price. So glorify God in your body."

Do we glorify God by what we put *in* our body? Do we glorify God by what we put *on* our body? Do we glorify God by what we *expose* our body to?

A temple! If people would think of the body as this temple, wouldn't that take care of a lot of problems of our day—abuse, harassment, alcoholism, smoking, anorexia, gluttony, sexual deviations, and all kinds of excesses? Can we do such to a temple?

Thank you, Lord, that I am fearfully and wonderfully made. Help me in all I do to remember that my body is a temple and You want me to glorify You. Amen.

19

Worship
(Psalm 84)

Do you have a longing in your heart? Do you wonder where to turn to satisfy that longing? Are you lonely—are you friendless—are you seeking for fulfillment?

Psalm 84 by the sons of Korah states: "How amiable are Thy tabernacles, O Jehovah of hosts! My soul longeth, yea even fainteth for the courts of Jehovah; my heart and my flesh cry out unto the living God" (ASV).

I hope you have a longing that will bring you into God's house to worship Him. He can satisfy your longings. He asks you to come to Him in order that you might be blessed and then you in turn can bring blessings to others.

We all need a church home where we can feel welcome and our needs can be met. Here we can have fellowship in the communion of saints. Here too we can use our talents so that the church can be built up. Here we can receive strength to live each day for the Lord.

Then we can say as the Psalmist ends this Psalm: "No good thing does the Lord withhold from those who walk uprightly, O Lord of hosts, blessed is the one who trusts in Thee."

Lord, help us to bring unto You and Your church those who have a longing in their hearts. Amen.

20

We Saw It!
(Matt. 4:16, 28:16–20. Luke 24:28–35,
John 20:18–20, 20:26–29, Acts 4:20, 9:27,
26:12–13, 1 John 1:1)

In this day and age, various events are caught on video. A TV program suggests that individuals who have caught something interesting on video can send it to a program called, "We saw It!" Actions and events can be verified by what ordinary people have seen and recorded.

The Scriptures too speak of people who could say, "We saw it!" or "We saw Him!" Some would not believe, but those who did believe were blessed and were promised eternal life. Philip found Nathanael and said to him, "We have found Him of whom Moses and the prophets wrote." Mary Magdalene, running away from the tomb, found the disciples and excitedly exclaimed, "I have seen the Lord!" The two on the way to Emmaus hurried to Jerusalem to the disciples and exclaimed, "We saw Him, talked with Him, and our eyes were opened when He broke the Bread." John writes in the First Epistle: "We saw it, and testify to it . . that which we have seen and heard we proclaim to you."

Have you seen, have you heard, have you believed, do you go and tell?

Lord Jesus, having seen and heard, help us to proclaim the good news to everyone we meet. Amen.

21

Great Work

I am doing a great work and I cannot come down. Why should the work stop while I leave it and come down to you?

—Nehemiah 6:3

Nehemiah was cupbearer to Artaxerxes, King of Persia. A discouraging report about Jerusalem came to Nehemiah. With the permission of the king, Nehemiah went to Jerusalem. The walls and gates of Jerusalem needed to be rebuilt, and Nehemiah was able to get the people to work. A conflict arose from neighboring officials. They asked Nehemiah to come down to meet with them, but Nehemiah knew they meant mischief and harm with intent to stop the building. Nehemiah tells them he is doing such a great work that he cannot come down to them. So finally the wall is finished and Jerusalem resettled.

Whatever work we have to do, if it does not go against God or do harm to our neighbor, is a great work. We must not give in to the enemies who want us to come down to them.

Students are doing a great work in preparing for future schooling or positions. Don't come down to drugs, smoking, guns, illicit sex, abuse, violence or even such things as cheating, lying, laziness. Making the most of educational opportunity is great work.

Those employed have a great work to do and should be thankful for that work. Think of the many who do not have jobs or positions and long to have work.

The work of witnessing for Christ, our Savior, is so great a work that we dare not let anyone or anything interfere with it.

Dear Lord, help us to honor all legitimate work and so do it to Your honor and glory. Amen.

22

Wait

I wait for the Lord, my soul waits, and in His Word I hope, my soul waits for the Lord more than watchmen for the morning.
—Psalms 130:5–6

Waiting seems so difficult. We are impatient people. We want the answer right now. We want the cure and healing right away. Why should it take so long? We live in hurry-up days. We long for immediate answers to prayer. Doesn't God hear?

Waiting and delaying are written large in the life of God's people. Read the faith story in Hebrews 11. We might also call it the waiting chapter. Think of what Noah must have experienced in building the ark. People ridiculed him, no doubt, when this huge boat was being built on dry ground. Job agonized in pain and accusations from his friends. Would deliverance come? You can recall others in God's Book who were exercised in their faith by waiting for God to fulfill His promises or lift their burdens.

Are you seeking answers to prayer? Are you looking for a certain position to open up for you? Are you hoping to be accepted by a certain college or university? Are you concerned about a loved one? We could go on and on.

"Wait for the Lord; be strong and let your heart take courage; yea, wait for the Lord" (Ps. 27:14).

"From of old no one has heard or perceived by the ear, no eye has seen a God besides Thee, who works for those who wait for Him" (Isa. 64:4).

Lord God, grant us the grace to wait for Your guidance and blessing. Amen.

23

Fear
(Deut. 6:1–3, Prov. 3:7, Prov. 1:7, Job 28:28, Ps. 33:8, Luke 1:50, Matt. 27:54)

Dr. Martin Luther writes in the *Small Catechism,* in his explanation to each of the commandments: "We should fear and love God . . . "

There is such a thing as a healthy fear. This fear is necessary in life. Such fear keeps us from acting foolishly. Parents try to instill this healthy fear in their children so they will not run out into a busy street filled with traffic or accept candy or a ride from a stranger.

Have we lost our healthy fear toward God? Or do we think we can be in a buddy-buddy relationship? The dictionary speaks of fear as "a mixed feeling of reverence and wonder." Also in defining awe, we are told it "refers to a feeling of fearful or profound respect or wonder inspired by the greatness, superiority, grandeur of a person or thing."

Young people often use the word "awesome" these days. Do they use it correctly?

The Scriptures teach us to fear and love God as we think of His greatness along with His goodness to us.

May we pray with the hymn writer, F. W. Faber, who wrote in 1849 the following:

Oh, how I fear Thee, Living God!
With deepest, tenderest fears,
And worship Thee with trembling hope,
And penitential tears!

Yet I may love Thee too, O Lord!
Almighty as Thou art,
For Thou hast stooped to ask of me
The love of my poor heart! Amen.

24

Look and Live
(Num. 21:4–9, Isa. 45:22, John 3:14–15, Rom. 10:13)

There is an interesting story from mythology that has to do with healing. One day Mercury found two snakes engaged in mortal battle. He touched them with his wand. At once they coiled themselves neatly and quietly around his wand. He liked the effect so well that he commanded them to stay there forever. Since Mercury was the god of physicians, such an emblem was chosen as a fitting symbol for them. It is called a Caduceus.

The Christian church has a different emphasis for this emblem. The Israelites in their wilderness journey became impatient and murmured against God and Moses. So the Lord sent fiery serpents to bite the people. Then the people came to Moses and confessed their sin against the Lord and against Moses. They asked Moses to pray. The Lord told Moses to make a fiery serpent and put it on a pole. So Moses made a bronze serpent, put it on a pole, and those bitten could look at this bronze serpent and live.

Jesus, in talking with Nicodemus, says the story of Moses and the serpent with the rebellious people fits into what He (Jesus) must face. As the Son of man, He too would be lifted up, and if people looked to Him, they would live. Look and live—receive eternal life.

Lord Jesus, we thank You that You were lifted up on the Cross for us because we had sinned. Help us to continually look to You that we may live. Amen.

25

Aspire
(The Book of Hebrews, Matthew 6:33)

"When you want something better, Aspire." Ford introduces a new car with air bags to protect what's really important, the ad says. This new car has been given a three-year, 36,000-mile bumper to bumper warranty, so you can stop worrying about the little things. Ford says "Aspire" is a new car for anyone searching for something better.

Do you aspire for something better in your life? Is there something better? Is there anything better in this world? The Bible tells us in 1 John 2:15–17 that we are not to love the world or things that are in the world. As Christians we are in the world but not of the world.

Where do we turn with our aspirations? The writer of the Book of Hebrews tells us that we can aspire to a better life through a personal fellowship with God through Jesus Christ. In Christ we can experience the grace we need for every circumstance and situation in life so we don't have to worry about the little things. The writer of Hebrews says Jesus is the author and perfecter of our faith so He can really protect what is important to us.

For anyone searching for something better, seek to know Jesus Who is a better messenger, better leader, better high priest, a provider of a better convenant with better promises, a better sanctuary and better sacrifices. He promises us a better life of faith, hope, and love.

Thanks to You, Jesus, we can aspire to something better and You are the One Who can satisfy our aspirations. Amen.

26

Weights
(Heb. 12:1, 1 Cor. 10:23, 24, & 31, Rom. 15:3)

Those who run races in contests in school, marathons, or in the Olympics have to discipline themselves. Those in speed skating find a demanding race. Winning the race must stand absolutely first. Everything else has to be secondary, and the racer must be willing to drop that something else as soon as it becomes a weight. An athlete who wants to be crowned the victor will not let personal pleasures stand in the way.

There are many things in life that in themselves may not be sin but can become weights in the Christian life. As we give ourselves to running the race of the Christian life, we must consider what might hinder us. Sometimes people are concerned about conduct in life. What is right for me to do? Can a Christian rightfully do such and such? It may vary with individuals. We need to ask ourselves—will the company I keep, the books I read, the TV I watch, the pleasure I participate in, the habits of eating, drinking, sleeping, etc., assist or hinder me in running the Christian race? If they become weights, they must go.

Lord Jesus, so live Your life in and through us that there will not be weights to hinder us in living our Christian life to God's glory. Amen.

27

Obsolete!
(Heb. 8:13, 2 Cor. 5:17, 1 Cor. 11:25, Rev.
21:5, Rom. 6:4, Isa. 43:19a)

It's amazing the changes we can experience in a lifetime. If we think of the office, we note that the electric typewriter replaced its cumbersome predecessor, the dictaphone made Gregg shorthand obsolete, the computer and word processor took over from the electric typewriter. On the farm the tractor and other machines took over from the horse. As for the kitchen and other places in the home, you can think of much that has been made obsolete by the new. For example, now you can bake bread without using the conventional oven.

Did you know that Jesus also came to make something obsolete? We know that all that has been made obsolete served very well in its day. So it was in God's realm too. The old covenant with its animal sacrifices pointed to salvation secured by the grace of God. But the new covenant is based upon a better sacrifice—the once for all offering of Christ Himself. Under the new covenant, we can put our trust in the actual person of Jesus Whose atonement for us on Calvary makes all things new.

As a part of this new covenant, Jesus instituted what we call "the Lord's Supper." Here we fellowship together, receive His forgiveness and the strength to live the "new life," which He came to bring.

Thank You, Jesus, for establishing the new covenant making the old obsolete, thereby making it possible for us to walk in newness of life. Give us strength to so live and to share our new life with others. Amen.

28

How Much Can You Take?
(2 Cor. 11:24–33, John 1:10–11, Matt. 13:53–58. Matt 10:38, Matt. 16:24, Gal. 5:11, Matt. 26:36–46, Luke 22:39–53, Joshua 1:5, Matt. 28:20, Jer. 23:3, 1 Cor. 10:13)

The speaker at my Augustana College graduation was the late Dr. Fredrik Schiotz, at that time executive secretary of the Commission on Younger Churches and Orphaned Missions of the National Lutheran Council. His challenging message to us was, "How Much Can You Take?" He wanted to alert us to what we might have to face in the world beyond college.

Today in our lives, we have to face difficulties, decisions, distresses, and even achievements. Young people, especially teens, may often wonder and say to parents or each other, "How much do I have to take?" Today we hear that many teens commit suicide because they can't take it anymore. Statistics state that more and more young people run away from home because they can't take it anymore.

All of us have difficult days to face, and we need to turn to the Lord. Jesus has promised that He will never leave us or forsake us.

We need to live in the Scriptures to find God's promises, which will bear us up in the midst of trials.

Dear Lord, we thank You that You know what it is to face trials, temptations, difficulties in life. Help us to turn to You for comfort and strength for each day. Amen.

29

Rocks
(Ps. 40:1&2, Ps. 62:5–7, 1 Cor. 10:4, Isa. 51:1)

The study of history is fascinating. To dig into the past can unveil many secrets. William Faulkner writes: "The past is never dead, it is not even past. History is a continuous river of time; in past events, are rocks that help you keep your feet dry."

Have you ever walked through a shallow stream of water and stepped from rock to rock? As a child you probably thought that was such fun if you could stay on the rocks!

There are many rocks of the past that can help to keep our feet dry. The rocks of our heritage: family heritage—hometown heritage—heritage of our country. Think of the heritage left by our Founding Fathers for this country. How we need to reexamine the rocks upon which this country was built and reestablish some of the values that were set forth.

Then there are the rocks of our Christian heritage. The greatest Rock is Christ. We sing, "On Christ the solid Rock I stand—all other ground is sinking sand." The church is built on Jesus the Christ—the Savior, the Redeemer, the Way, the Truth, the Life. In Him is life for us.

Dear Jesus, thank You for being the Rock. Thank You that Your church is built on You, the Rock, and that we are part of that church. Amen.

30

Joy
(John 15:11, Ps. 16:11, Isa. 35:10)

In the fifteenth chapter of the Gospel of John, Jesus speaks about being the true vine. He speaks about the fruit-bearing Christian. This is not possible unless the Christian abides in Christ. Abiding in Him makes fruit bearing possible. Christ bears the fruit in and through us through the work of the Holy Spirit. Jesus at one time said that His followers would do greater works than He did because He was going to the Father. The Holy Spirit would take what was of His and declare it to the followers of Jesus. Thus the Father was to be glorified.

Then in Christ His followers would receive a great benefit. Jesus said, "My joy may be in you, that your joy may be full."

Joy—what a wonderful experience. Joy that leads to singing. Joy that makes the face light up bringing smiles. Joy bringing lightness to one's step. Joy that causes one to see positive and countless possibilities. Joy that eliminates living in the negative. Joy that enables one to climb when it was thought impossible. Joy enabling one to tackle a task and finish it with a deep sense of accomplishment. All this because Jesus gives us His joy. He is the enabler.

Lord Jesus, thank You for giving us joy and enabling us to do that which glorifies the Father in heaven. Amen.

31

Walls
(Prov. 18:11, Acts 23:3, Eph. 2:4, Exod. 14:22, Isa. 26:1–4)

Walls—walls can symbolize something good or something evil. Walls are sometimes built to keep those safe who are within. Walls are sometimes built to keep what is without—out! In recent times we experienced a wall that caused terror by day and terror by night. Many who tried to escape over that wall were killed. Soldiers guarded it. President Reagan said, "This wall must come down." It was the Berlin Wall, and he did see it come down. What rejoicing as that wall crumbled!

We often build walls around ourselves. We may think that these definitely are for our safety. We definitely feel certain elements, people, customs, ideas must be kept from entering in. Walls of hatred, prejudice, self-righteousness, fear, imagination, blame, guilt, indecisiveness can become strong and we are imprisoned.

But there is God—we can be thankful for all the times we can know about God's intervention. But now through Christ Jesus, these walls can be broken down and we can be released from the imprisonment! What rejoicing! Jesus breaks down the dividing wall of hostility.

If we do need a wall at some time, God will provide for us as He did for Israel when He divided the Red Sea and the Jordan, making the waters like a wall at their sides so they could walk on dry land.

Dear Lord, help us break down the walls that are not within Your will. Amen.

32

Abstain
(1 Thess. 5:22, Gal. 5:16–24)

Today has become the day of permissiveness. "Everyone is doing it" is the cry. To be "in," you have to go along with the crowd, which indulges in all kinds of fleshly desires. Satisfaction is one's right—if it isn't given freely—just take it.

In the midst of this, it is good to hear that some young people are for abstinence. Abstain from drugs, from alcohol, from sexual intercourse until marriage. "True love waits" is their cry. Some young people are signing a pledge to abstain. How wonderful! More power to them.

Certainly Christians of all ages should abstain. Saint Paul gives many practical exhortations in his writings. He writes, "Abstain from every form of evil." In his writings, he gives lists of the desires of the flesh that can become addictions and bring ruin upon an individual, his family, his work; yes, his very life. Paul also gives lists of the fruit of the Spirit, which should characterize the Christian life. The directives for our life are in the Scriptures.

Lord Jesus, live Your life in and through us so that we will abstain from evil and live the fruit of the Spirit. Amen.

33

Name
(Ps. 8:9, Pro. 32:1, Hos. 12:5–6, Phil. 4:8 (ASV))

What's in a name? Think about it.

When I was growing up, I loved to read. Every Wednesday I would go to the public library in our town and take out two books. I'd read those, and then on Saturday, I'd take them back and take out two other books. There was a novelist, Grace Livingston Hill, who wrote many books, usually with a Christian slant to them. One time I read one of her books that had a girl named Effie. My name is Effie. She wrote that in Philippians 4:8 it states one of the characteristics to think upon is that of "good report." She said the word in Greek for that expression is one from which the name Effie comes. So from then on, I always wanted to be "of good report."

Do you know what your name means? One special meaning is that God has called us by name to be His.

God has a name—yes, many names. He is the great I Am, the Alpha and Omega, the Almighty. Jesus said that He, Jesus, is the Good Shepherd, the Light of the World, the Way, the Truth and the Life, the Healer, the Resurrection and the Life.

You might like to go through the Scriptures to find all the names attributed to our Lord. Then live a life of praise in honor of that name.

Jesus, thank You for telling us Who You are. May we love and honor Your name. Amen.

34

Memorial
(Josh. 4, Mark 14:9)

It is good to remember. Sometimes it is good to erect a statue, a building, or something tangible for people to see that will cause people to remember. At the present time, plans are in the making for a memorial to be erected at the entrance to Arlington National Cemetery in Washington, D.C. This memorial will be in honor of all women deceased or living who have served or are serving in the military forces of our United States. Lest we forget—may a grateful nation honor not only men but the women who have served in all wars or who are serving in peacetime.

Joshua, who led the Israelites into the promised land, was told by the Lord to set up a memorial. The stones of the memorial would recall what God had done in the past as well as to commemorate the crossing of the Jordan. This was also to help Israel when facing future difficulties to look to God who had formerly been their deliverer.

Today as believers we need to erect some stones of remembrance to thank God for what He has done for us. As human beings it is good to commemorate what God has done in various times in our lives.

Heavenly Father, we thank You for all that You have done for us in the past. Help us to remember and enable us to teach the coming generations of Your goodness and power. Amen.

35

Secure
(Rom. 8:31–39)

We read and hear much about living and being secure in these days and establishing security for old age. Young couples are urged to begin early to set aside a certain amount of money so that their children can be sure to secure an education. Young workers are urged to invest early for a secure retirement. Those who are struggling to make it, to pay all their bills and get on a secure footing are urged to prepare a budget and stick to it.

All these suggestions are good for us. It is important to have our house in order to be able to meet daily requirements. But beyond this, there is something else that is more important—our relationship to God.

The Apostle Paul says that if God is for us, who can be against us? Even if they are against us, God is greater than they and can keep us secure in His love. If you know Jesus as your Savior, that is the most important fact for your security. Nothing can separate us from the love of Christ. "Neither life, nor death, nor angels, nor principalities, nor things present, nor things to come, nor powers, nor height, nor depth, nor anything in all creation, will be able to separate us from the love of God in Christ Jesus our Lord."

Now, that's being secure!

Lord Jesus, we thank You that we are secure in Your hands. Enable us to help others to lay hold of this security. Amen.

36

"Take with You Words"
(Hos. 14:1–2)

Hosea was a prophet in the Northern Kingdom during the reign of Jeroboam. Instead of putting their trust in God, the leaders of the Northern Kingdom courted the favor of Assyria and Egypt. Hosea calls upon Israel to repent. Hosea's doctrine of God's love is rich, fair, and tender, making also his doctrine of repentance full and gracious. He calls Israel to "take with you words and return to the Lord."

There may be many times when we should take with us words and return:

If we have neglected the Lord and His House of Worship, we need to return.

If we have sinned against a brother or sister in the Lord, we need to take with us our words. Words to express sorrow and to ask for forgiveness.

If someone has lost a loved one, take with you words from the Scriptures that can comfort and heal the grief.

If someone has accomplished or achieved a goal and is honored, take with you congratulatory words. Rejoice in the joy of others.

You can probably think of other instances in which to take with you words.

Hosea writes about God's promise of blessing if Israel will repent and return. We too can be richly blessed in our relationship with others.

Thank You, Lord, that You have given us words in order to come to You and words to use in our relationship with others. Amen.

37

The Re-Decade
(Acts 2:18, Ps. 103:5, James 4:7, Ps. 107:2, 2 Tim. 2:8, Phil. 4:4, 2 Tim. 1:6)

This might well be called the re-decade. We are called on to re-cycle, re-organize, re-define, re-finance our mortgage, re-direct our thinking, re-evaluate our country, re-duce—take off those pounds.

All of these re-experiences might be good for us to follow and develop.

The Lord in His Word has many "re" words, which it would be well for us to take note of and make a part of our life.

Repent—turn away from evil and turn to God. Every day must be a turning to God as Dr. Martin Luther reminds us.

Resist—"resist the devil and he will flee from you." Young people must "just say no" to what has become the enticement "everyone does it." Older people need to resist the temptation to be judgmental, to seek after riches above God, to be overcome by marital troubles.

Remember—remember Jesus and all that He suffered for us. Remember how He has led you in the past. Remember promises and vows—pledges that you have made.

Rejoice—"rejoice in the Lord always, again I say rejoice," says Saint Paul.

Redeemed—"let the redeemed of the Lord say so!"

Dear Lord, help us who are redeemed, to rejoice and witness to our faith. Amen.

38

My Great Tower of Strength (Ps. 18)

The summer of 1974 provided me with a special privilege—travel to Norway. It was a time to praise God for His marvelous creation as we viewed towering mountains, thundering waterfalls, peaceful valleys, and gorgeous flowers. As the majestic mountains came into view, I could just hear the Augustana College Choir (1953) singing, "O God, Hear My Prayer," by Gretchaninoff, based on Psalm 18. Verse 2 of that Psalm states, "The Lord is my rock, and my fortress, and my deliverer, my God, my rock, in whom I take refuge, my shield, and the horn of my salvation, my stronghold."

Did you note the many "Mys?" Let Him be your personal God—He is your tower of strength.

How thrilling to see churches from the past preserved in Norway and how they seemed to be the focal point in the center of the towns. In Voss, a brochure proclaimed, "We are still filled with wonder that our old church [dedicated in 1277] escaped the bombs of the last war [World War II] which left most of the town in ruins, and we are greatly thankful that the house of God has recovered the glory of its past." God proved His faithfulness and His strength to those people in the trying times of World War II.

O God, how wonderful You are. We bow in awe and wonder at Your marvelous care in preservation of Your church and its people and in realizing that You are our tower of strength. Amen.

39

Alone or a Quiet Place (Matt. 14:23, Luke 6:12, Luke 9:28, Mark 6:46)

Jesus took time off! Yes, even though He was concerned about people and mingled with them, He disappeared from them at times. He preached, He taught, He healed, He fed the crowds, He raised the dead. But He did not forget His relationship with His Heavenly Father. He left the crowds, went to the hills, was alone and there prayed. He sought a quiet place, a place away not only from the crowds but even from His disciples.

We too need to take time off. Get away from the hustle and bustle. We may find a quiet time at home or at church when worship services are not on. Sometimes we may need to get away for a longer time. A good place to do this is Mount Carmel on Lake Carlos near Alexandria, Minnesota. Here you can partake of nourishing, stimulating food for the physical body as well as the spiritual body. There is time for fellowship with others, and there is time to retreat and be alone.

The directors, Sonja and Rev. Johann Hinderlie, describe it this way: "a place where spiritual nourishment, physical release and mental stimulation happen in a relaxed unpretentious atmosphere." "A Christ-centered community with fellowship for all ages where the Gospel is experienced."

Take time to grow in your spiritual life as you spend time in meditation and prayer.

Lord Jesus, help us to take time off away from distractions to communicate with You. Amen.

40

White as Snow!
(Isa. 1:18)

Can there be anything more beautiful than a winter wonderland? In the fall the trees shed their leaves and stand so stark and gray. The lawns lose their luscious greenness. But God often clothes the trees and the grass in beautiful, sparkling whiteness. After a snowstorm He brings out the sun with its brightness and warmth and makes one feel like singing. The children can't wait to get out their sleds and ski equipment and get out into that snow. Adults too join in on the fun, and it is a happy time.

We may have a fall-like experience in our lives. Because of the work of the evil one, we may have dark, bleak days. It may seem as if the sun will never shine.

In the midst of this depression, God comes and speaks to us: "Though your sins be as scarlet, they shall be as white as snow." As white as snow—newfallen snow! How wonderful God is! He cares about us—He forgives and restores us so that we can rejoice and sing again. A chorus we have learned says:

Though your sins be as scarlet
They shall be as white as snow.
Though they be red like crimson
They shall be like wool.

Kind Heavenly Father, we thank and praise You for forgiveness. Thank You for the white, white snow and its message to us. Amen.

41

Prayer for Wisdom
(1 Kings 3:5–14, James 1:3–7)

Knowledge is good. Many are seeking knowledge in various fields in educational institutions here and abroad. These institutions are dedicated to seeking out the truth and imparting this to the students. Students are challenged to dig deeply into the mysteries of all life, seeking for answers in order to make their everyday lives more secure and enjoyable.

It is hoped that along with acquiring knowledge, the student will also seek wisdom to make proper use of this knowledge.

Solomon in a dream was asked by God, "What shall I give you?" Solomon made a solemn prayer in humility before God. What he asked for was an understanding mind to rule the great people of Israel. God commended him on his prayer and granted him wisdom and even what he had not requested, riches and honor.

James, in his Epistle in the New Testament, states that if anyone lacks wisdom, he can ask for it of God Who gives "generously and without reproaching." We need to pray that God will grant us wisdom for our lives.

Kind Heavenly Father, we come in awe and wonder to Your throne. We sing in one of our hymns, "Thine endless wisdom, boundless power and awful purity." Almighty as You are, yet we dare to approach You seeking wisdom for our daily life. Amen.

42

No Cast Away

Feed My lambs. Feed My sheep. Follow Me.

—John 21:15–19

Simon Peter said to his friends, "I am going fishing."

His friends said, "We will go with you."

These men who were the disciples of Jesus had been fishermen before they answered the call of Jesus to follow Him. Now after Jesus' death and resurrection, frustrated by all the events of "these past days," fishing seemed appealing.

Jesus came to them and even prepared breakfast for them on the beach.

When they had finished breakfast, Jesus questioned Peter. "Simon, son of John, do you love Me?" Peter, the one who had vowed allegiance to Jesus in the presence of the other disciples, was the one who denied that he even knew Jesus. Even now, no doubt, he remembered that look Jesus gave him that caused him to weep bitterly.

At this encounter with Jesus, Peter is not scolded. Jesus could have said, "After what you did, I can't use you." No, Jesus did not cast Peter aside but gave him work to do in the Kingdom.

How thankful we can be that Jesus can use us too. He asks us to follow Him and bear fruit.

Thank you, Jesus, for forgiveness and for opportunity to serve You. Amen.

43

Bound—Unbind!
(John 11:38–44, Gal. 5:16–6:10)

We have heard many sermons on Jesus' raising Lazarus from the dead. Jesus prayed to God so that people gathered at the grave would be led to believe that Jesus was sent from God. After Lazarus came out from the grave, Jesus gave a command to the Jews who stood by: "Unbind him, and let him go."

John then writes that many of the Jews who had seen what Jesus did believed in Him, but some went and talked about Jesus to the Pharisees.

Note that Jesus says, "Unbind him." In those days they bound the hands and feet with bandages before placing them in the grave. Only Jesus could give him life, but others were called on to unbind him.

Jesus is the One Who saves and we can bring others to Jesus to be saved. Christians who have new life might still be bound by some of the desires of the flesh. We can help to unbind them. Pray for them and as Paul states in Galatians, if they are overtaken and bound by a sin, those who are spiritual are to restore them in a spirit of gentleness. Unbind them—do good to them that Jesus may be glorified and others, seeing it, may believe.

Lord Jesus, thank You for including us in the work of the Kingdom. Enable us to serve in helping to unbind those who are bound. Amen.

44

Take Him Back
or
Forgiveness and Reinstatement
(Phil. 21)

Today we often hear of persons who have been wrongly removed from a place of employment. Oftentimes this may be done to remove a worker who has been with a company a long time and therefore commands a larger salary than a new, younger worker. Sometimes such persons have been reinstated, given back pay, and are assured of full acceptance by the company.

The Apostle Paul writes an exquisite letter to Philemon. Onesimus, Philemon's slave, had run away. He had made his way to Rome and been converted to Christianity by Paul. Paul would have liked to retain him as his servant, but he felt he should send Onesimus back to Philemon.

Paul's letter to Philemon reveals Paul's ability of Christian persuasion and graciousness. He goes all out for Onesimus. "Receive him as you would receive me. If he has wronged you at all, or owes you anything, charge that to my account." Read the Book of Philemon.

Christianity makes a difference in how we relate to others. Can we go all out on behalf of another person? Can we write letters on behalf of someone we can help?

Lord Jesus, help us to be forgiving and give assistance to others. Enable us to be living examples of the grace we have received. Amen.

45

Restore
(Eph. 6:1–5, James 5:19–20)

These days we often hear testimonies of individuals who have been on drugs, into alcoholism, or some type of addiction who have been restored to life as it was before these addictions.

Chuck Colson even said on TV that he was thankful for Watergate and jail because through that experience he came to know Jesus Christ and now was living to bring glory to Him Who saved him from death and shame.

Paul admonishes those of us who are spiritual to restore anyone who has been overtaken by some sin. He also challenges us to look to ourselves lest we also be tempted.

James, in his Epistle, tells us that if we bring a person back from the error of his ways, we will save that person's soul from death and will cover a multitude of sins.

What a wonderful challenge! Let's be in the business of restoration—the recycling even of individuals. Most of us probably can't be on the front lines in this effort, as we don't have the training and expertise, but we can pray for those on the front lines doing the restoration and speak well of them. I think of a young lady in Lutheran social service up in the Twin Cities who was saving young girls from the streets. I praise God that He has people willing and able to do that!

Thank You, Lord, that we can be restored, if we stray. Grant us grace, wisdom, and strength to help those wandering from the truth. Amen.

46

Stand in the Breach

Therefore He said He would destroy them—had not Moses, His chosen, stood in the breach before Him, to turn away His wrath from destroying them.

—Psalms 106:23

Moses, His chosen one, stood in the breach. He turned to God on behalf of his people so they would not be destroyed.

We too have been chosen and saved from destruction. Is there someone for whom we should stand in the breach?

A wayward son or daughter.
A sick child.
A member of the family outside of Christ.
A sick member of the congregation.
A person who has lost a loved one.
A lonely person.
A young person faced with decisions.
A homeless person or family.
A nation filled with factions at war with one another.
A person facing serious surgery.
A person with a disability.
A pastor who has many responsibilities.
A church staff person who gives all for the church.
A volunteer who serves the Lord.
A jobless person seeking work.
A missionary facing many problems.

You can probably add to the list.

Lord Jesus, give us the strength to stand in the breach for many who need us. Amen.

47

Robbing God?
(Mal. 3:6–12)

There is much talk these days about the economy. Retailers are seeking to up their receipts from previous years. Consumers are wanting more and more things, products, and equipment to make life easier. Computers now take care of all kinds of tasks. Machines of various kinds are made to equip the kitchen. Now you can even bake bread without using your conventional oven.

It is not wrong to have these things, provided they do not take all our funds, even those we may have put aside for God. "You may be robbing Me," says God.

But God says more than that. He says to bring all the tithes into His storehouse and put Him to the test. If all the tithes come in, God will open the windows of heaven and pour out such a blessing that it will be overflowing. Not only that, but nations who see this being done will call us blessed and we will be a land of delight. Fulfilling God's request should also be an answer to the gambling problem.

Do we want blessing, delight, and joy? Do we want to witness to God's goodness to us? If we do, then let's do what God asks.

Heavenly Father, thank You for Your abundant provision for us and Your wonderful promises. Help us to be obedient servants in Your Kingdom. Amen.

48

Evil or Good
(Gen. 50:15–21)

The story of Joseph in Egypt and the dealings with his brothers
is very moving. Joseph said to his brothers, "Fear not, for am I
in the place of God? As for you, you meant evil against me; but
God meant it for good, to bring about that many people should
be kept alive, as they are today. So do not fear; I will provide for
you and your little ones. Joseph forgave his brothers and dem-
onstrated this to them.

It may be that we too may suffer evil at the hands of kin or
other people. We too must have a forgiving spirit and pray that
God will work it out for our good as well as that of other people.
When God does work it out for our good, then we must find ways
to do good to others.

We are only hurting ourselves if we have resentment, anger,
or an unforgiving heart. As we think about how God in Christ
has forgiven us and blessed us in spite of our trials, how can we
do less than forgive? It will be our opportunity for reconciliation,
forgiveness, and restoration.

*Lord Jesus, thank You so much for Your great forgiveness to
us. Enable us to forgive others and restore them to favor in Your
sight. Amen.*

49

Fitly Spoken
(Prov. 25:11, Prov. 15:32–3, James 3:1–12)

A couple who had been married for ten years had continually been extremely busy, she as a writer and he as a professor. Now finally they were going on vacation to Arizona. How exciting! But the anticipation was spoiled by a silly argument before they left. At the beginning of their vacation, it seemed like a great gulf was developing between them. The wife prayed for God's help. God reminded her of the argument and the need of forgiveness. God seemed to say, "Take with you words." So she did and from that time on they had a wonderful vacation.

The Apostle James speaks about the tongue and the damage it can do. Read the third chapter of the Book of James.

Then instead of allowing the tongue to get you into trouble, turn your tongue over to the Lord. Fill your mind with the good words from the Scriptures, from hymns, from devotional books. Think before you speak. Guard that tongue so that your words will be fitly spoken, filled with love, not hate, jealousy or arrogance. Let Jesus work miracles through you by what you say.

Guard Thou the lips from sin
The hearts from shame,
That in this house have
Called upon Thy Name. Amen.

—J. Ellerton (1866)

50

The Discipline of Darkness
(Ps. 112:4, Ps. 139:12, 1 Pet. 2:9)

The days of World War II brought various disciplines of darkness into the lives of many people. A brother of mine who served in the Pacific theatre of that war was plunged into physical darkness. While in the Philippines, he lost his eyesight through the explosion of a Japanese land mine. The rehabilitation was difficult not only for him but also for the members of his family. It was quite an experience for me, his sister, to grapple with that darkness.

In the midst of that darkness, we were able to walk in the light—the light of God's Word. We hung on to the practical truth of what had often been said: "Never doubt in the dark what God has told you in the light."

Often Christians may go through prolonged and painful periods of spiritual darkness. Even Saint Paul, the great giant in Christian faith, writes in 2 Corinthians chapter 1: "We were utterly, unbearably crushed that we despaired of life itself... but that was to make us rely not on ourselves but on God."

In experiencing darkness, we may feel that God has forgotten us or forsaken us. Then we need to search the Scriptures and find again those rich promises. He knows. He cares. We can trust Him to bring us back into the light.

Lord Jesus, thank You that You are the light of the world. Help us to trust You daily and to walk in the light so that in You our darkness can be overcome. Amen.

51

Triumph
(2 Cor. 2:14)

It was fascinating to watch the winter Olympics games in Lillehammer, Norway, in February 1994. Many hours of practice had been clocked by skiers, speed skaters, hockey players, figure skaters, pair skaters, dance skaters, bobsledders, and others. The days of triumph came for some, and they stood proudly to receive their medals and were exhilarated by the playing of the national anthems of their countries.

God wants us to triumph in our Christian life, and He provides that experience of triumph for us. Read His Word, let Jesus live His life in you and through you. Surrender your life to Jesus—it must be a daily thing. Dr. Martin Luther said that the new man must daily come forth and arise.

Saint Paul exhorts us to give thanks to God because He says that He in Christ always leads us in triumph. We are commissioned by God, empowered by Christ, and indwelt by the Holy Spirit. Our bodies are the temple of the Holy Spirit. God wants us to triumph—so rejoice in His provision.

Our Heavenly Father, we come to You in awe and adoration for Your gracious provision for us. Help us each day to live in the triumph You are providing us. Amen.

52

Love
(Heb. 13, 1 Cor. 12:31—Ch. 13, 1 Cor.
14:1, John 15:12–13)

The Apostle Paul in 1 Corinthians 12 talks about the specific gifts that the Spirit gives to Christians. Then he goes on to say that he will show "a still more excellent way." Then he writes that beautiful chapter on love, namely, 1 Corinthians 13. This chapter can be read again and again, and if possible, memorized.

We are part of the body of Christ, and we are commanded to love one another. Christ is the source of love and can enable us to love even our enemies so that we can pray for them. The early Christians were noted for the love that they showed to one another. Love would solve all the problems in our relationships with the members in the church. Love could solve differences in the home, difficulties with teenagers, and right relationships between employer and employee.

God the Father loved the Son; the Son then used His Father's love as a model for His love to His disciples. He gave Himself for them and not only for them but also for us. The disciples then loved one another and passed the love on to all in His church.

Lord God, thank You for loving us so much that You gave Your Son for us. Teach us to love as You have loved. Amen.

53

"If My People!"
(2 Chron. 7:14, Deut. 14:2, Acts 11:26)

On the *60 Minutes* television program on CBS, Alexander Solzhenitsyn appeared recently, giving some views on America. He seemed inclined to believe that America is losing its spiritual and moral fiber. The U.S.A. is beset with many problems and Russia more so than the U.S. He was going back to Russia after living here for eighteen years. He said he was going to travel and talk with the people there in hopes that he could be of help to them.

As Christians of the United States of America, we need to be aroused to action and to prayer that our land may be healed and redeveloped to the moral fiber with which it began. Our forebears came to this land with hopes and dreams of founding a nation where God would be considered the ruler and the people His believing subjects. It was thought that here their children could be raised without oppression. Liberty and freedom would prevail in a democracy.

We need to pray for this land that we will not forget from whence we have come. We need to get back to the Ten Commandments, to living moral lives, to honoring the family, the church, and to studying the Scriptures.

Christ our Savior came that we might have life. We are called by His Name—Christ-ians—followers of the Christ. If we humble ourselves, pray, seek God, turn from evil, God will hear and heal our land.

Kind Heavenly Father, thank You for calling on us to turn from evil and to turn to You. Bless our beloved U.S.A. Amen.

54

Require
(Mic. 6:8, Deut. 10:12–13, Luke 12:48,
Heb. 6:1, Eph. 4:13–16, Col. 1:28, 1 Cor.
14:20, Rom. 12 and 13)

Many people are writing résumés today. People are seeking jobs or positions of responsibility. Some have been relieved of positions because of layoffs at companies. Some have sought to meet the requirements of certain positions after going back to high school, college or graduate school. Now they have to present themselves as having met the requirements of education, experience, and attitude. Can they meet the reuqirements? Can they get the jobs in question?

What does God require? Beyond believing that Jesus is the Christ, the Son of the Living God, are there any requirements? Yes, the Scriptures contain many passages describing the requirements of Christian conduct. You might read the passages given above and then use cross-references given in your Bible to find many more passages for living the Christian life.

As you read, don't get discouraged, but turn yourself over to Jesus. He has said that He will live His life in and through you. Study John 15. We cannot bear fruit by ourselves, but as we abide in Jesus, fruit will abound. Let Him live in and through you and requirements will be met. You will be amazed by what He can do.

Dear God, thank You for what You require and for the provision that you have made. Amen.

55

The Birth of the Messianic King!
(Isa. 9:2 & 6, Luke 2, John 3:16–17)

One can hardly ever read the ninth chapter of Isaiah without seeming to hear Handel's *Messiah* majestically proclaiming, "Unto us a Child is born, unto us a Son is given." What a spiritual experience George Frideric Handel must have had as he set the Scriptures to music!

We may not have that gift of music, but our hearts too can be set to music when we dwell upon the Scriptures. As we read about the birth of the Messiah King and come to know that it refers to the Lord Jesus Christ as God-Man, our whole being will rejoice in God our Savior.

Then as we proceed into the New Testament, reading Luke 2 and then on to John 3:16–17, we can claim this Son of God as our Savior.

The Epistles of the New Testament give us encouragement and directives on how to live the Christian life and to share this story of the Savior with others.

This Prince of Peace, so named in Isaiah, gives us peace in our hearts, a peace that passes our understanding and gives us the message of peace to share with one and all.

Kind Heavenly Father, thank You for loving us so much that You sent Jesus to be our Savior and the King of our lives. Amen.

56

Hang On!
(1 Cor. 16:13–14, Rev. 3:11)

These days we have some of our strong beliefs questioned. We belong to the communion of saints. We are citizens of two worlds—the here and now and the Kingdom to come. We are called to sanctification—to grow in our Christian life. The Holy Spirit works in our lives, calling us to live the life of saints. We must not forget to study and live in the Word, attend Holy Communion, and live a life of prayer.

Saint Paul urges us to be watchful, to stand firm in our faith, to be courageous and strong. How we need these exhortations today when there are those who try to discredit the Word, thinking they can live lives that go against the teaching of the Scriptures. Young people whom we read about are willing to experiment in many ways for which they will have to pay a high price.

God calls us to "hang on." Don't let go. Abide in Him and let His Word abide in You.

The Apostle John, writing to the church in Philadelphia in the Book of Revelation, commends the church for keeping the Word and not denying the Name of Jesus. He exhorts the church to "hold fast what you have, so no one may seize your crown."

Heavenly Father, thank You for Your Word. Help us to hang on and not let go of the doctrines that we have learned. Amen.

57

Provoke
(Heb. 10:24, Titus 3:8, Heb. 13:1, 1 Thess. 5:11 & 15)

Many times the word *provoke* has negative connotations. We may be provoked to anger. We pray that we will not be provoked to jealousy.

The Bible also uses *provoke* with the negative emphasis. The Israelites traveling in the wilderness, guided by God, Who met all their needs, still forgot His mercies to them. The Psalmist says, "They tested Him again and again, and provoked the Holy One of Israel." The Apostle Paul, in writing the great love chapter in 1 Corinthians, states that love is "not provoked."

It may be a surprise then to note that the writer of Hebrews uses the word "provoke" with a positive, urgent connotation: "Consider how to provoke one another to love and good works." Some translations use "stir up" or "encourage." Perhaps "provoke" gives a much stronger emphasis. Love and good works—that's what it's all about for the Christian. Christ has done all for us and we are His.

The prayers for some of the Sundays in Advent and Pentecost seem to fit in with this word *provoke*, but use instead "stir up." We'll use a composite from these prayers as our prayer:

Stir up Your power, O Lord, and come. Give us strength in our conflicts and shed light on our path. Stir up, O Lord, the wills of Your faithful people to seek more eagerly the help You offer through our Lord Jesus Christ. Amen.

58

Equip
(Eph. 4:11–16, Col. 3:5–17, 1 Thess.
4:9–11, 1 Thess. 5:12–22)

When in the fall we think of children going back to school, we know they need to be equipped with certain supplies. It is interesting to note that in Sioux Falls, "The Banquet" is accepting school supplies to be used to equip children and older students so that they can go back to school. Their parents, who might find it difficult to afford the purchase price of these supplies, are happy that the community is willing to equip them.

It is good to be well equipped for what one may have to do. In the church, too, the Bible speaks about the importance of equipping the saints. This may come as a surprise. Aren't the pastor and staff there at church to meet my needs and the needs of all the other parishioners? Yes, they are. But the pastor and staff are there to equip the believers to do their ministry. Parishioners should gladly submit themselves to receive this equipment. The Apostle Paul in Thessalonians also exhorts the believers to "respect those who are over you in the Lord and esteem them very highly in love because of their work."

Heavenly Father, grant us grace to live and work in harmony in our churches so that the ministry that You would have us do can be done to Your honor and glory. Amen.

59

New Thing
(Isa. 42:9, 43:18–19, Ps. 149:1, 1 Cor. 11:25, Rev. 21:1–7)

It is important to remember to give thanks for blessings of the past but not to forget to look forward to what might be better. A hymn for the new year states:

With grateful hearts the past we own,
The future, all to us unknown,
We to thy guardian care commit,
And, peaceful, leave before thy feet.

—P. Doddridge (1755)

The Israelites were instructed by God through Moses to remember that they were in bondage in Egypt but then were set free. He cared for them. They were not to forget these blessings but to pass on to their children an understanding of how graciously God had dealt with them. They were also to look to God for the new thing that He would do for them.

A new thing—many times change is difficult to face. When we are young, change is often exciting even though it may be faced with mixed feelings. Sometimes it's great to go to a new school, meet new people, get away from home. It's fun to have new clothes. Exciting to go to a new restaurant and sample foods of another culture—new tastes.

When Jesus came into the world, God did a new thing. With Jesus we received a new covenant, a new name—Christian, a new church, a new life.

Lord Jesus, thank You for the new life You have given us for now and for eternity. Give us grace to follow You and accept the changes that are part of the newness of life. Amen.

60

Do Good—Not Harm

They angered him at the waters of Meribah, and it went ill with Moses on their account.

—Psalms 106:32

The Israelites in the wilderness made life difficult for their leader Moses. God had chosen him to lead the people and his was a huge assignment.

Sometimes congregations find fault with their pastors and perhaps this is not justified. We need to hold them up in constant prayer and esteem them highly for their great calling.

So often we are told not to blame others for the various circumstances in our lives. Sometimes these may be our own faults, but at other times, they may be what others are doing to us. Nancy Kerrigan of ice-skating fame was victimized by being struck on the leg. This came as a complete shock to her. She questioned, "Why?"

The second great commandment is to love our neighbors as ourselves. Dr. Martin Luther, in the *Small Catechism*, states it this way: "We should fear and love God, and not falsely belie, betray, backbite, nor slander our neighbor, but excuse him, speak well of him, and put the best construction on all he does."

Love does no ill to one's neighbor.

Kind Heavenly Father, keep us close to You so that we do not cause others to sin but rather help them to live a life pleasing to You. Amen.

61

Trials
(Job 23:10, James 1:2, Job 19:25. Read all of Job.)

Job had three friends who heard of all the evil that had come upon him, and they came to console him. They sat with him seven days and seven nights without speaking. Then when they spoke, they tried to make Job out to be a liar and hypocrite and the evil plight he was in a just consequence of his sin.

Job does not buckle under the accusations of his friends. He maintains, "But He knows the way I take; when He has tried me, I shall come forth as gold." And he also said, "For I know that my Redeemer lives."

The Lord told Eliphaz that he and his friends had not spoken of Him what is right as Job did. The Lord told the friends of Job to go to Job, make an offering for themselves, and Job would pray for them.

The Book of James tells us to count it all joy when we meet various trials. May we learn to turn to the Lord at such times.

As friends of those who are suffering various trials, it is good to be concerned about them. It is good to visit them to encourage them. But we had better watch our tongues, as the Book of James tells us. May we not condemn or bring charges as the friends of Job did. Rather may we build one another up and pray for one another.

Heavenly Father, thank You that You do not let us be tried beyond our strength, but will see us through to victory. Amen.

62

The Word of God Endures
(Isa. 40:8)

Everything seems to change so fast. Is there nothing we can hold on to? The whole world seems to be shaking. Countries that seemed to be stable are falling apart. People who have lived peacefully together are now fighting one another.

Isaiah reminds us that the grass under our feet withers; the flower we so admired also fades. Where can we turn? Isaiah gives the answer: "The Word of our God shall stand forever." This was the motto of two educational institutions I attended—The Lutheran Bible Institute of Minneapolis and Augustana College of Sioux Falls. The education at these institutions is greatly to be desired, but the greatest of all is to know the Word of God. "All Scripture is inspired by God and profitable for teaching, for reproof, for correction, and for training in righteousness, that the man of God may be complete, equipped for every good work" (2 Tim. 3:16–17).

Kind Heavenly Father, thank You for Your Word. Help me to read it, memorize it, store it up, and live according to it. Amen.

63

Grace
(2 Cor. 13:14)

What do you think of when you hear the word "grace"? Grace at meals, royalty spoken of as His Grace, gracious people, and a God of grace?

How would you understand the grace of our Lord Jesus Christ? I think of Dr. Martin Luther who in his days as a monk lived in fear of the living God. He experienced what the writer of Hebrews says: "It is a fearful thing to fall into the hands of the Living God." A God of wrath was what he knew, and he did everything he could to placate an angry God.

But then—searching the Scriptures, he found that he was justified by what Jesus had done for him. He heard Jesus say that he was saved by grace.

Only after tasting the grace of the Lord Jesus did he come to know a loving God, a God Who so loved that He gave—He gave His only Son to die that Martin might live!

Having experienced the grace of the Lord Jesus and basked in the love of God, he then began to enjoy the fellowship of the Holy Spirit. What a change in his life! The Holy Spirit opened the Scriptures to him, led him to become a prolific writer of hymns, of studies in the Scriptures and a translator of the Scriptures so that others might come to know this grace, love, and fellowship.

Thank You, Lord, for grace, which abounds to us. Amen.

64

Crushed

For we do not want you to be ignorant brethren, of the affliction we experienced in Asia; for we were so utterly, unbearably crushed that we despaired of life itself!

—1 Corinthians 1:8

Who could write words like this? None other than the great Apostle Paul. Could even such a man of God be so crushed? Yes, even he. I think it is a great help to us to know that someone so close to the Lord Jesus could suffer so and even be driven to despair.

Do you feel crushed? Do you even despair? Take heart and search the Scriptures, and you too will be able to say with Paul, "Blessed be the God of all comfort who comforts us in our affliction so that we may be able to comfort those who are in any affliction with the comfort we ourselves are comforted of God" (2 Cor. 1:3–4).

Lean on the Lord, tell Him you need Him every hour. Plead with Him till you receive the help and comfort He can give. Ask Him to give you the willingness and ability to comfort others.

Thank You, kind Heavenly Father, that You are a comforting God. Give us the grace to give comfort to others. Amen.

65

Praise

I will give thanks to the Lord with my whole heart; I will tell of all Thy wonderful deeds, I will be glad and exult in Thee, I will sing praise to Thy Name, O most high.

—Psalms 9:1–2

I love Thee, O Lord, my strength. The Lord is my rock and my fortress, and my deliverer, my God, my rock in whom I trust, my shield, and the horn of my salvation, my stronghold.

—Psalms 18:1–2

The Lord is my light and my salvation; whom shall I fear? The Lord is the stronghold of my life, of whom shall I be afraid?

—Psalms 27:1

How great it is to give praise to our God. We may feel weak and inadequate in ourselves, so we must look up to God. Praise Him and He will make a difference in our day.

Think of these words and admonitions from the Psalms; be glad, sing praise, give thanks. Consider who God is: my strength, my rock, my fortress, my deliverer, my shield, my stronghold, my light, my salvation.

Dear Lord, help us to lay claim to all that You are for us. Live out Your life in us that the world may know You and the power of Your resurrection. Amen.

66

Delivering Goodness

I waited patiently for the Lord; He inclined to me and heard my cry. He drew me up from the desolate pit, and out of the miry bog, and set my feet upon a rock, making my steps secure. He put a new song in my mouth, a song of praise to our God. Many will see and fear, and put their trust in the Lord.

—Psalms 40:1–3

In this Psalm David acknowledges God's delivering goodness. David had suffered but now was restored.

There may be times when we need to wait patiently for the Lord. We need to cry unto Him and when deliverance comes, praise Him for it. This will not only be a blessing to us, but God can use it as a blessing to others to make Himself known. As David said, "Many will see and fear and put their trust in the Lord."

Corrie Ten Boom, who was imprisoned by the Nazis during World War II, found ways to praise the Lord and many have been blessed by her testimony.

Lord, help us to wait patiently for Your deliverance in our trials. When deliverance comes, help us to praise and glorify You so that many will see it and be glad. Amen.

67

Boldness

Let us therefore draw near with boldness unto the throne of grace, that we may receive mercy, and may find grace to help us in time of need.

—Hebrews 4:16 (ASV)

Timid, fearful, guilt-ridden, ashamed—how do I dare approach a Holy God?

Do you sometimes feel that way? Then look to Jesus. He tells us that we can draw near to the throne with boldness.

The disciples felt down at the time of the crucifixion and immediately after. Confusion, questions, fear as to what to expect engulfed them. Then Jesus came to them and before His ascension, He told them to wait for the Spirit.

After the outpouring of the Holy Spirit, the disciples became bold. In the Book of Acts, we read that Peter and John healed a lame man. They were then imprisoned and later brought before the Sanhedrin and questioned. The result? They were set free. "Now when they beheld the boldness of Peter and John, and had perceived that they were unlearned and ignorant men, they marvelled; and they took knowledge of them that they had been with Jesus" (Acts 4:13).

You were sealed by the Holy Spirit at baptism. Jesus says the Holy Spirit will take of what is His and declare it unto us. Jesus also tells us we can approach a holy God in His Name and receive mercy and grace to live as God would have us live.

Dear Jesus, grant us boldness to approach the throne of grace. Amen.

68

Gethsemane

As Christians we suffer distress, discouragement, darkness, and danger at various times in our lives. We might call these Gethsemane experiences. At times we know not what to do, but thanks be to God, we can cry to Him.

In the church where I grew up, the altar picture was of Peter, who prayed one of the shortest, yet most effectual prayers. A Gethsemane experience? Peter cried, "Lord, save me" (Matt. 14:30).

Hadn't he asked for this? He was in the shelter of the boat, but he asked Jesus to bid him approach Our Savior on the water. Jesus had said, "Come." When he looked to Jesus, Peter was able to walk, but then doubt came and with it sinking into the water.

So all of us as Christians have our times much like Peter. It may be like a Gethsemane experience for us.

All those who journey, soon or late,
Must pass within the garden's gate;
Must kneel alone in darkness there,
And battle with some fierce despair,
God pity those who cannot say;
"Not mine but Thine," who only pray;
"Let this cup pass," and cannot see
The purpose in Gethsemane.

—Ella Wheeler Wilcox

Lord Jesus, help us learn from our Gethsemanes. Amen.

69

Follow Jesus—on Your Own (John 21:21–23)

You're on your own now! Guess we've heard that quite often. It can be great, but it can be a little scary too. If we have been in the shelter of our home, or with others, and supported by them, it is sometimes difficult to be on our own.

It is good to have family and close friends we feel comfortable with. How good to have a friend we can rely on when problems and troubles arise. It is good to have those with whom we can share our joys and good times. Peter and John had shared many experiences together as the inner circle with Jesus.

We need to be involved with other people, but there are times when we have to be on our own. Jesus says this to Peter when he, Peter, referred to the Apostle John and said, "Lord, what about this man?" Jesus said to Peter, "If it is My will that he remain until I come, what is that to you? Follow Me!"

"Follow Me" is what Jesus says to us too. Even if others may not follow Jesus, we who have said we believe, must go it alone with Jesus. If a friend relates to Jesus differently than you do, go ahead and follow Jesus as He directs you.

Follow, I will follow Thee, my Lord,
Follow every passing day,
My tomorrows are all known to Thee.
I will follow all the way.

70

No Excuses Accepted
(Exod. 3 & 4, Jer. 1:4–10, Isa. 6:1–13)

Who am I that You should call me? They won't believe me. I am not eloquent—in fact I get tongue-tied. Send some other person. I do not know how to speak. I am too young. I am too old.

Have you ever made similar excuses when you have been asked to do some task in the church or even the community?

The excuses given above were given to God when He called men to serve. God had a plan and He knew who He wanted to have carry out those plans. God also provided the means by which His plans could be carried out. He equipped them with what they needed. He said He would work through them.

Jesus said too, "You did not choose Me, but I chose you and appointed you." When Jesus chooses you, He also equips you. Step out on His promises, live in His Word, ask for His guidance. It an be an exciting experience to see what He can do through you. Open yourself up to Him—let Him work out His plans in your life—it will be an extraordinary adventure.

Lord Jesus, help us to surrender all to You. Live out Your life through us. Amen.

71

Living Stones
(Eph. 2:20–22, 1 Pet. 2:4–8)

Palestine is a stony country, I am told. Fields may have to be cleared of stones preparatory to cultivation.

Stones were used in many ways. They were used in palaces, fortresses, for dikes about vineyards, for bridges, paving streets, and many other uses. Stones—huge ones—were used at the entrance of tombs.

The Israelites often consecrated a single stone as a memorial. Stones were used to build an altar to worship God. "Then Samuel took a stone and set it up between Mizpah and Jeshanoh and called its name Ebenezer, for he said, 'Hitherto the Lord has helped us' " (1 Sam. 7:12).

A living stone is a stone in its natural condition, strong, sound, resilient, and not disintegrating. We as followers of Christ are living stones. We have been given life by Christ, who is the Chief Cornerstone. Peter says that as living stones we are to be built into a spiritual house. Jesus has made us alive together with Him, and He calls us to be a fortified wall against that which is evil.

Lord Jesus, we thank You that You have forgiven our sins and made us alive. As living stones, help us to take our stand with You against all evil. Amen.

72

Shield
(Ps. 28:7, 18:30, 144:2, Eph. 6:16)

"Shields were used by all nations of antiquity. The Israelites employed a larger and a smaller kind. The larger kind, translated shield, buckler, target, belonged to the heavy spearmen and lancers. The smaller shield, rendered shield or buckler, was carried by archers. Shields were of various shapes—round, oval and oblong. They were commonly made of several thicknesses of leather or of wood covered with leather" (*The Westminster Dictionary of the Bible,* John D. Davis, Ph.D.).

In light of the above, the people of Bible times were familiar with shields. Shields were used to protect those engaged in warfare.

The writer of many of the Psalms, namely David, spoke of the Lord as his strength and shield. David from his youth had depended on the Lord as that shield. He writes a song of praise to the Lord when he is delivered from the hand of Saul.

The Apostle Paul speaks in Ephesians of the church's warfare. He admonishes us to put on the whole armor of God and take "the shield of faith to quench the flaming darts of the evil one."

Dear Lord, increase our faith so that we may be strong in our warfare. Amen.

73

Give Thanks
(Ps. 92:1, 75:1, 105:1, 107:1, 111:1, 136, 138, 139)

When we are growing up, we are often reminded to give thanks. Mothers usually remind a child when they receive even a cookie, by saying, "What do you say now?"

In Old Testament times, among the many offerings to God was a thank offering. The thank offering was in recognition of unmerited and unexpected blessings.

The writers of the Psalms write often about giving thanks to God for all His wonderful deeds. Thanks were to be given to God for His steadfast love, His mercy, and His deliverance.

David, the Psalmist, writes about God's omniscience and omnipresence and omnipotence. He extols the God of all creation, who formed the marvelous body of the human being, giving him rational faculties.

In light of what God has done, shouldn't we give thanks? Then when we think of Jesus, Who was willing to do the Father's will (and thereby give Himself for us!), need we be asked, "What do you say now?"

Kind Heavenly Father, we do not know how to give thanks adequately but we bow before You to thank and praise You for all that You are and for all You have done for us. Amen.

74

Refuge
(Ps. 71:1, 34:8, 46:1–3, 27:5, Isa. 4:5–6,
Joel 3:16–17)

Quite recently on TV, we heard about a young couple who, traveling with their baby, took a side road on a trip and got caught in a snowstorm. They walked for a long way until finally the man decided to go on alone. They had found a cavelike formation and the young lady with her baby was able to crawl in for refuge. Here she and her baby survived. The husband was finally able to get help, and rescuers came to the place of refuge to aid this woman and her baby.

It seemed like a miracle! How wise of them to seek refuge! God has promised refuge for us too. We can flee unto Him for hiding us in the midst of storms. Just think of what He promises:

He will hide me in His shelter in the day of trouble (Ps. 27:5).
Happy is the person who takes refuge in Him (Ps. 34:8)
Though mountains shake, though waters roar, God is our refuge and strength (Ps. 46:1–3).
A shade from the heat, a shelter from storm and rain (Isa. 4:6).
The Lord is a refuge; a stronghold (Joel 3:16).

Shouldn't we praise the Lord continually for His great provisions for us?

Kind Heavenly Father, thank You for being our refuge and strength, our stronghold. Amen.

75

Decisions

Multitudes, multitudes in the valley of decision! For the day of
the Lord is near in the valley of decision.

—Joel 3:14

Day after day we make decisions. Some may seem very small,
and some loom very large.

How do we make decisions? We may study the circumstances. We may go to guidance counselors, to parents, to
friends, to pastors. All of these actions may be important, But
most important would be to follow the example of Nehemiah who
said, "So I prayed to the God of heaven." Prayer and the study
of God's Word should be a part of a Christian's decision-making.

Jesus Himself sought a way to escape from the crowds to go
to a quiet place to pray. Jesus often talked with His Father that
He might do God's will. We are reminded of Jesus' high priestly
prayer in John 17 and His prayer of agony in the Garden of
Gethsemane. Here the decision became clear: "not my will but
Thine."

*Kind Heavenly Father, lead us and guide us along life's
way—for without You we cannot but stray. Amen.*

76

For Us
(Mark 9:28–41, Luke 9:51–56)

The disciples of Jesus were very privileged. They were with Jesus, heard Him preach and teach, witnessed His miracles, listened to His parables, and were equipped to do service for the Kingdom. But during these days with Jesus, they were schooled by Him. They had much to learn. Sometimes they were impulsive and suggested actions that were contrary to what Jesus thought should be done. In these instances He rebuked them. When people would not receive Jesus, the disciples were even so rash as to ask Jesus if they should bid fire to come down to consume the people. At another time they saw a man casting out demons in Jesus' name and wanted to forbid him this because he wasn't one of them. But Jesus said no because anyone "who is not against us is for us."

We too need to learn that there are others besides ourselves in the Christian church. We do not need to compromise our belief or leave our doctrines. We, as Lutherans, have much to offer.

Thanks be to God that many Christian organizations are working for the salvation of souls. Let's be happy for all the people who are not against us but for us and pray for them in their endeavors. What a power Christ could become if all Christians surrendered their lives completely to Him.

Lord Jesus, thank You that You are for us and You have many people who also are for us. Help us also to be for them. Amen.

77

Water of Life
(John 4:7–30, John 7:38, John 3, Rev. 22:17)

Water—how precious it is! Water—clear, cool water to drink. Water for bathing, water to wash clothes, water even for fun, like water slides and swimming. How refreshing!

But water can also cause havoc. Many experienced this in the great Midwestern flood of 1993. Levees failed and water roared like a waterfall along the streets and into basements. Many had to leave homes by boat. Houses and churches were filled with mud and debris.

People in other states sent bottled water for those in devastated areas to drink. Water to drink—how satisfying!

In the Scriptures we read about water. The water of baptism when God claims us as His own in the name of the Father and of the Son and of the Holy Spirit. Life-giving water—new birth—spiritual birth! Jesus speaks of the water of life, which He will give, saying that the one who receives it will not thirst again. Jesus invites us to come, to drink, and to live!

Lord Jesus, thank You that You have and are the Water of Life. Grant us a thirst for this life-giving water so that we will come to You and be satisfied. Amen.

78

Youth
(1 Tim. 4:12, Eccles. 12:1, Jer. 1:6, 1 John 2:14b)

Our newspapers and TV bombard us with stories about youth gang activity, drug abuse, alcoholism and guns and knives in school. We are almost led to think that all teens are evil and enmeshed in all wickedness.

But there is another side to our youth story. Many who are involved in sports belong to the Fellowship of Christian Athletes. Others are involved with Sports Spectrum, an organization supporting sports and the Christian faith, which broadcasts on radio and publishes *Sports Spectrum Magazine.* There are also teens who find time and energy to give volunteer service in their communities. Some volunteer on a regular basis. A special day is set aside in some communities each year to recognize the work of youth volunteers.

"In 1993, Lutheran Brotherhood received special recognition at the White House for its ongoing support of Youth Community Service" (*Lutheran Brotherhood Bond*—Spring 1994, page 11).

There are various references to youth in the Scriptures. Youths are encouraged to live Godly lives and to give faithful service and be an example even to their elders.

We hear that young people in high schools are having prayer gatherings at flag poles at schools and Bible study at school outside of school hours. Other organizations are allowed to use school premises, so it was decided that Christian youth could not be denied the use of those same premises.

Lord Jesus, thank You for youth who are dedicated to You. Help us to encourage them, pray for them, and speak well of them. Amen.

79

Bread of Life (John 6:35, John 6:25–34, Jer. 37:21, Eccles. 11:1)

Today many cry for bread. It's amazing that there are so many homeless and hungry people in America. A highly cost-effective way to ensure a healthy start for America's children, the Supplemental Food Program for Women, Infants, and Children (WIC) provides supplemental foods, nutrition education, and medical screening to low-income pregnant women, new mothers, infants, and children up to age five.

Communities are having food collections to add to other distribution centers for the hungry. Organizations like the Boy Scouts periodically collect food. Churches take monthly turns in collecting food for the needy of the community.

This is good. We need to satisfy physical hunger. But there is another hunger that must be satisfied—the spiritual hunger. What in life has meaning? What can I do about it?

Jesus has the answer. In fact, Jesus not only has the answer, He is the answer. He is necesssary to sustain the spiritual life of the believer. He says that the hunger in us will be satisfied, for He is the Bread of Life. He fully and forever satisfies our needs of the heart.

Lord Jesus, help us to help feed the hungry in body and soul that their hunger might be satisfied. Amen.

80

Everlasting Arms
(Deut. 33:27, Ps. 98:1–2, Isa. 52:10, John 12:37–38, Mark 9:33–37, Mark 10:13–16)

The human body is a miracle. It has so many wonderful parts. As we think of hands and arms, we wonder how we could ever do without them. To lift a child, to hug and thereby show our love. To lift burdens, to hold onto things, to throw a ball, to swing a golf club. You can add to the list.

Often in wartime, soldiers may have arms that are wounded or may even have to be partially amputated. Recently we heard of a young farmer who lost his arms in a farm accident but saved them and had them reattached.

God too is pictured to us as having arms, arms to embrace us and arms to uphold us, arms to give us the victory. How comforting to know that "underneath are the everlasting arms of God."

Jesus is pictured as One Who took little children up into His arms and blessed them. Jesus touched people and healed them. He invited people to come to Him and to take His yoke upon them. Jesus carried the Cross for us and spread His arms out on the Cross for us. By what He did, we are saved.

Heavenly Father, we thank You that by Your holy arms You have gotten us the victory. You gave Your Son upon the cross that we might be saved. Hallelujah! Amen.

81

Build
(Matt. 16:18, Acts 20:32, 1 Thess. 5:11, Luke 20:17, 1 Cor. 14:12, Ps. 118:22)

These days we hear about building activities and organizations that are of great help to people. Habitat for Humanity is focused on providing homes for low-income families who otherwise might not be able to own a home. Those who get together to provide money, tools or skills to build, enjoy good fellowship and a sense of satisfaction and accomplishment when the work is completed.

Mission Builders are retired carpenters, construction workers, and other volunteers who help ELCA congregations construct new buildings. Mission Builders have completed forty-five construction projects since the program was launched in 1988.

What a wonderful way to build up the church. The congregations who benefit are enriched as well as those involved in the building.

Our faith is built on Christ Jesus, Who said He would build His church on the confession of Peter: "You are the Christ, the Son of the Living God." Built on Jesus the Christ, we are encouraged to build one another up in our Christian life. Christ is the Rock on which we build. This must be our focus. This must be our witness. There are forces that would take away our faith. We sing, "On Christ the solid Rock, I stand. All other ground is sinking sand." We must take our stand.

Lord Jesus, we thank You that You are the Rock. Help us to take our stand and seek to build one another up in the faith. Amen.

82

Hands
(Isa. 9:17, 41:10, Num. 11:23, Exod. 4:2,
Ps. 104:27–28, Lam. 3:41, Acts 11:19–21,
Ps. 24:4)

Diligent, creative hands in Mission Viejo, California, responded to a huge undertaking. The members of Mount of Olives Lutheran Church learned a new skill. More than 250 people were involved. They learned the *dalle facet* method to prepare stained-glass windows for their church. It became a spiritual experience. Making new friends was also an unexpected plus.

What is that in your hand? Hands can be creative for the good of someone else. What comes from your hand can heal, can bring joy, can give surprises, can help the hungry and homeless.

The Scriptures speak of hands—God's hand on our behalf. His hand is stretched out still to rescue individuals and to bring salvation. His hand and arm are spoken of as getting Him the victory. The victory is in the giving of His Son, Jesus the Christ, to bring salvation to all who will receive Him.

Kind Heavenly Father, thank You that Your hand of salvation is stretched out still. Help us to grasp that hand. Then help us to use our hands in creative ways to bring glory to Your name. Amen.

83

Cloud of Witnesses
(Heb. 11, Heb. 12:1–2, Heb. 10:36, 1 Cor. 9:24–27)

Isn't it amazing how many people travel many miles to take in the Rose Parade in Pasadena preceding the football game? Most athletic events bring crowds. On TV the stadiums are shown with every seat taken at football games, baseball games, and hockey. On golf greens, crowds follow the golfers as they tee off and cheer them when they make excellent putts.

The Scriptures remind us that we too have a great cloud of witnesses. The eleventh chapter of Hebrews relates various examples of faith. We are reminded of individuals who endured in spite of seemingly overwhelming odds.

In our own day and age, many examples of faith come to mind in our own families and acquaintances. Many others we have read about, like Albert Schweitzer, musician, theologian, and physician, who left lucrative position possibilities in Germany to go to Africa to heal the sick; and the prisoner martyr of World War II, Deitrich Bonhoeffer.

It is good to look to the giants of the faith. Hebrews 11 exhorts us to "lift your drooping hands and strengthen your knees, make straight paths for your feet." The Christian race is not something to be taken lightly. The witnesses are cheering us on. In Christ we can endure. We can look to Him who is the pioneer and perfecter of our faith.

Lord Jesus, help us to keep our eyes fixed on You as You encourage us in our Christian race. Amen.

84

Peace
(John 14:27, Rom. 5:1, Rom. 14:19, Eph. 2:14, 15, 17, 1 Pet. 2:11, Col. 1:20, Col. 3:15, Heb. 13:20)

Perhaps one of the most amazing peace processes that happened recently (1994) was held in Norway. Norway's efforts as a secret mediator in building trust between the PLO and Israeli representatives was almost unbelievable. Some negotiations were held in farmhouses and others in hotels in Oslo. Johan Jorgen Holst, then Norway's minister of foreign affairs, said he was convinced the family atmosphere broke down barriers of suspicion and got the two sides on good terms.

Paul writes in Ephesians also about an amazing peace process of bringing about peace between the Jews and the Gentiles. Paul reminds the Gentiles that they should remember that at one time they were "separated from Christ, alienated from the commonwealth of Israel . . . having no hope and without God in the world." "But now"—how Christ changed things. Jesus is the peacemaker Who has "broken down the wall of hostility . . . that He might create in Himself one new man in place of the two, so making peace."

This peace process must continue. Christ has bought peace by the blood of His Cross. This is the good news we must pass on to others so Christ can bring peace to their hearts and we can rejoice.

Lord Jesus, thank You that You are our peace. Help us to be peacemakers all the days of our life. Amen.

References

Bainton, Roland H., *Here I Stand.* Bergenfield, NJ: A Mentor Book, New American Library, 1978.

Congressional Record. 94th Cong., 1st Sess., 1975, Vol. 121, pt. 92.

Evangelical Lutheran Augustans Synod, *The Hymnal.* Rock Island, IL: Augustana Book Concern, 1925.

Explanation of Luther's Small Catechism, abridged edition. Minneapolis, MN: Augsburg Publishing House, 1927.

Ford, Gerald R., President. Proclamation. "National Day of Prayer," 1975.

Halley's Bible Handbook. Grand Rapids, MI: Zondervan Publishing House, 1973.

Harper Study Bible, Revised Standard version. New York: Harper and Row, 1952.

Holy Bible, The, American Standard version. New York: Thomas Nelson and Sons, 1901.

Lutheran, The. Minneapolis, MN: Augsburg Fortress Publishers.

Lutheran Book of Worship. Minneapolis, MN: Augsburg Publishing House, Board of Publication, Lutheran Church in America, Philadelphia, PA, 1978.

Lutheran Brotherhood Bond, 625 Fourth Ave. South, Minneapolis, MN, spring 1994.

Luthern Hymnary, The. Minneapolis, MN: Augsburg Publishing House, 1927.

Thanks-Giving Square Foundation, 3141 One Main Place, Dallas, TX, 75250.

Walk Your Way to Fitness. Mayo Foundation for Medical Education and Research, 1992.

Webster's New World Dictionary. David B. Guralnick, editor in chief. William Collins Publishers, Inc., 1980.

Westminster Dictionary of the Bible, The. Philadelphia, PA: The Westminster Press, 1944.

About the Author

Effie Ruth Larson, daughter of Mr. and Mrs. Ed. O. (Ellen Marie) Larson, grew up in Clark, South Dakota.

She is now a retired associate in ministry of the Evangelical Lutheran Church in America (ELCA), having been certified and commissioned in the American Lutheran church (ALC), one of the predecessor churches of the ELCA.

Effie is a graduate of the Lutheran Bible Institute, Minneapolis, Minnesota. She is a magna cum laude graduate of Augustana College, Sioux Falls, South Dakota. Her graduate work was at Washington University, St. Louis, Missouri, and South Dakota State University, Brookings, South Dakota. Continuing education courses were taken while in her profession, such as summer conferences on theology and ministry at Augustana College, Sioux Falls, South Dakota, in 1979 and 1981. In 1983, she attended the summer conference on theology and ministry at Concordia College, Moorhead, Minnesota.

During her professional years, she served as payroll clerk at The Texas Company, Denver, Colorado; physical therapy technician in the Medical Corps of the Army of the United States; Girl Scout executive, Olympia, Washington; administrative assistant at Saint Olaf Lutheran Church, Austin, Minnesota, and Saint Stephen's Lutheran Church, West Saint Paul, Minnesota.

Effie currently lives in Sioux Falls, South Dakota, and is an active member of First Lutheran Church.